101 FA

MW01137765

FACTS ABOUT

CRISTIANO RONALDO

Essential Trivia, Quotes, and Questions for Superfans

FALCON FOCUS

THIS BOOK BELONGS TO

_____

TABLE OF CONTENTS

INTRODUCTION

Welcome to *101 Fascinating Facts About Cristiano Ronaldo,* an in-depth exploration of the life and career of Cristiano Ronaldo, a footballer whose name resonates far beyond the boundaries of the sport. This book is a celebration of Ronaldo's journey, one marked by extraordinary talent, relentless determination, and a record-breaking career that has set him apart as a global sports icon.

In these pages, you will uncover a rich mosaic of facts, stories, and achievements that paint a vivid picture of Ronaldo's rise from a humble beginning in Madeira to becoming a household name across the world.

INTRODUCTION

Each fact is carefully selected and crafted to capture the essence of Ronaldo's impact both on the football field and beyond.

Please note that the information, including statistics and records, presented in this book is current as of October 2023. As Cristiano Ronaldo continues his career, it's important to remember that these numbers may evolve. Ronaldo, an athlete known for his unwavering drive and ambition, is still actively contributing to the world of football and his legacy.

DID YOU KNOW?

Cristiano Ronaldo's full name is Cristiano Ronaldo dos Santos Aveiro. He was born on February 5, 1985, on the small island of Madeira, Portugal.

He was born into a humble family and is the youngest of four children of Maria Dolores dos Santos Aveiro and José Dinis Aveiro.

DID YOU KNOW?

Cristiano Ronaldo's father, José Dinis Aveiro, worked as a municipal gardener and was also a part-time kit man for Andorinha, the local football club where Ronaldo first played. José struggled with alcoholism and passed away in 2005 due to liver failure.

His mother, Maria Dolores dos Santos Aveiro, worked as a cook to help support the family. She played a crucial role in Ronaldo's life, encouraging his football talents and often taking him to training sessions and matches in his early years.

DID YOU KNOW?

Ronaldo's older brother, Hugo, has worked on projects related to Ronaldo's CR7 brand and museum.

———————————————

Cristiano has two older sisters, Elma and Liliana Cátia. Elma is involved in the family business, particularly managing Ronaldo's CR7 fashion brand, while Liliana Cátia, also known as Katia Aveiro, is a singer in Portugal and has released several albums.

DID YOU KNOW?

Cristiano Ronaldo was named after Ronald Reagan, a favorite actor of his father's, as his parents appreciated the name's strength and resonance long before Reagan became the President of the United States.

As a child, Ronaldo earned the nicknames 'Cry Baby' and 'Little Bee' from his family and friends; 'Cry Baby' due to his tendency to cry when his passes didn't lead to goals, and 'Little Bee' for his notable speed, a trait that continued to define his playing style throughout his career.

DID YOU KNOW?

At the age of eight, Cristiano Ronaldo started playing football, joining the amateur team Andorinha in Madeira, Portugal.

DID YOU KNOW?

At the age of 14, Cristiano Ronaldo was expelled from school after he threw a chair at his teacher, citing disrespect as the reason for his actions. Although this incident had negative consequences, it marked a significant turning point in his life. Encouraged by his mother, he channeled all his attention into soccer, a decision that ultimately propelled him to become an international sensation in football.

───────────────

At the young age of 15, Ronaldo underwent critical heart surgery to address his diagnosed condition of Tachycardia, a rapid heartbeat exceeding 100 beats per minute that posed risks of stroke or heart failure. As his mother recounted to the Daily Mail in 2009, doctors utilized a laser technique to cauterize the source of the issue, allowing for a swift surgery that saw Ronaldo leave the hospital by the afternoon of the same day.

DID YOU KNOW?

His professional football career began in 2002 when he debuted for Sporting CP in Portugal. He was just 17 years old.

In 2003, Ronaldo's exceptional talent caught the attention of Manchester United, leading to his signing for a then-record fee of £12.24 million for a teenager, marking his entry into the English Premier League.

DID YOU KNOW?

At Manchester, he became renowned for his signature move, the 'Ronaldo Chop,' a skillful step-over technique frequently used to outmaneuver defenders during matches.

DID YOU KNOW?

During his time at Manchester United, Ronaldo won three consecutive Premier League titles in the 2006-07, 2007-08, and 2008-09 seasons.

———————————————

In the 2007-08 season, Ronaldo played a pivotal role in helping Manchester United secure the UEFA Champions League title.

WHAT IS THE BALLON D'OR?

The Ballon d'Or (French for "Golden Ball") is an annual football award presented by France Football. It has been awarded since 1956, although between 2010 and 2015 it was merged with the FIFA World Player of the Year award and known as the FIFA Ballon d'Or. However, in 2016, the Ballon d'Or again became a separate award.

The award is given to the best male footballer in the world for the year, as judged by a panel of international journalists. Each journalist selects the top five players and points are allocated based on their ranking – the first receiving five points, the second four points, and so on.

Historically, the Ballon d'Or was restricted to European players playing in European clubs. However, this rule was changed in 1995, allowing non-European players to be eligible for the award as long as they were playing for a European club. In 2007, the award was opened to players of any nationality, regardless of the continent in which they played.

The Ballon d'Or is one of the most prestigious individual awards in football and is widely regarded as a symbol of excellence in the sport.

DID YOU KNOW?

Ronaldo clinched his first FIFA Club World Cup in December 2008 with Manchester United.

_____

He was awarded his first Ballon d'Or in 2008, recognizing him as the best player in the world.

DID YOU KNOW?

In 2009, Cristiano Ronaldo made a historic transfer to Real Madrid for a then-world record fee of £80 million, marking the most expensive football transfer at that time.

Ronaldo spent nine seasons with Real Madrid, during which he became the club's all-time leading scorer.

WHAT IS THE UEFA CHAMPIONS LEAGUE?

The UEFA Champions League, often referred to as simply the Champions League, is the most prestigious club competition in European football. Organized by the Union of European Football Associations (UEFA), the tournament has been a cornerstone of European club football since its inception in 1955, originally known as the European Champion Clubs' Cup or simply the European Cup.

The competition involves the top club teams from Europe's most competitive national leagues. Its format has evolved over the years and currently features several stages, including qualifying rounds, a group stage, and knockout rounds culminating in the final. The group stage pits teams in groups of four, with the top two teams from each group advancing to the knockout phase.

The Champions League is celebrated for showcasing high-level football and features many of the world's most renowned clubs like Real Madrid, Barcelona, Manchester United, Bayern Munich, and Juventus. Winning the Champions League is considered one of the highest honors in club football, symbolizing continental supremacy.

The tournament has become known for its iconic anthem, based on George Frideric Handel's Zadok the Priest, which plays before each game. The anthem and the Champions League logo have become symbols of the high quality and prestige associated with European club football's elite competition.

DID YOU KNOW?

During Ronaldo's time at Real Madrid, he won four Champions League titles.

_____

He was ranked third in the 'World Player of the Decade 2000s,' behind Lionel Messi and Ronaldinho.

WHAT IS THE COPA DEL REY?

The Copa del Rey (Spanish for "King's Cup") is an annual knockout football competition in Spanish football, organized by the Royal Spanish Football Federation. It was first held in 1903, making it one of the oldest football competitions in the world. The cup is contested by teams from various levels of the Spanish football league system, showcasing a wide range of talent and competition.

The format of the Copa del Rey involves a series of knockout rounds, traditionally starting with single-leg matches in the early rounds, progressing to two-legged ties in the later stages, and culminating in a single-match final. This structure allows for exciting and unpredictable matches, often leading to unexpected outcomes and thrilling moments in Spanish football.

Initially, the competition was mainly contested by teams from the top divisions, but it has since expanded to include teams from lower divisions, giving smaller clubs a chance to compete against the giants of Spanish football. This inclusion adds a unique charm to the tournament, as it allows for classic "David vs. Goliath" matchups.

The winner of the Copa del Rey is awarded a prestigious trophy and often earns a place in the UEFA Europa League for the following season, unless they have already qualified for the UEFA Champions League through their league position. This provides an additional incentive for clubs to perform well in the competition.

DID YOU KNOW?

Cristiano Ronaldo won his first trophy with Real Madrid during the 2010-11 season, securing the Copa del Rey. This victory marked an important milestone in his career with the club, as it was his first piece of silverware in the famous white jersey of Real Madrid. The final itself was a riveting spectacle, with Real Madrid facing arch-rivals Barcelona. Ronaldo's performance in the final was nothing short of spectacular, scoring a crucial header that secured the victory. This win not only brought an end to Real Madrid's 18-year Copa del Rey title drought but also set the tone for Ronaldo's subsequent achievements with the club.

WHAT IS SUPERCOPA DE ESPAÑA?

The Supercopa de España, or the Spanish Super Cup, is an annual Spanish football competition. Established in 1982, it traditionally pits the winners of La Liga, Spain's top football division, against the victors of the Copa del Rey, the national cup competition. The event serves as a curtain-raiser for the Spanish football season and is seen as an opportunity for the top teams in Spain to set the tone for the upcoming year.

Originally, the Supercopa de España was contested over two legs, with one match played at each participating team's home ground. However, the format has seen changes over the years. Since 2019, the competition has been expanded to include four teams - the winners and runners-up of both La Liga and the Copa del Rey - and is held in a single-round knockout format at a neutral venue.

The Supercopa de España provides an early-season opportunity for fans to witness a clash of Spain's football titans, often featuring high-profile matchups such as Real Madrid vs. Barcelona. These games are not only a display of high-quality football but also a showcase of the deep rivalries and rich history that characterizes Spanish football.

Victory in the Supercopa de España is highly valued, as it signifies triumph over some of the strongest teams in Spanish football. It is seen as a prestigious accolade and an early indicator of a team's form and potential for the season ahead.

DID YOU KNOW?

In the following season, 2011-12, Ronaldo secured his first La Liga title with Real Madrid.

The 2012-13 season saw Ronaldo winning the Supercopa de España with Real Madrid.

DID YOU KNOW?

He won his second Ballon d'Or in the
2013-14 season.

WHAT IS THE FIFA WORLD CUP?

The FIFA Club World Cup is an international men's association football competition organized by the Fédération Internationale de Football Association (FIFA), the sport's global governing body. Inaugurated in 2000, the tournament was initially held annually, then biennially, and again annually since 2005. It features the champion clubs from each of the six continental confederations, along with the national league champion from the host country.

The competition is structured as a small tournament with a few rounds, leading to a final that determines the world's top club team. The format typically includes a preliminary round, a quarter-final round, semi-finals, and the final. This format ensures that teams from different continents have the opportunity to compete against each other, making it a true test of global club supremacy.

Initially, the tournament faced challenges in establishing its significance in the football calendar, given the already packed schedule of top teams. However, over time, it has grown in prestige and is now highly coveted by participating clubs. Winning the FIFA Club World Cup is considered a great honor, symbolizing global dominance in club football.

The competition has seen representation from a wide array of clubs, showcasing diverse playing styles and football cultures. Traditionally, teams from Europe and South America have been more successful, reflecting the strength of football in these regions.

DID YOU KNOW?

In the 2013-14 season, Ronaldo also won another Copa del Rey and his second Champions League, setting a record with 17 goals in the tournament.

_____

Ronaldo received his third Ballon d'Or in 2014, along with his second FIFA Club World Cup in December of the same year.

DID YOU KNOW?

In 2016, he won his third Champions League with Real Madrid. He scored the winning penalty in the final against Atlético Madrid.

WHAT IS LA LIGA?

La Liga, officially known as La Liga Santander for sponsorship reasons, is the top professional football division of the Spanish football league system. Administered by the Liga Nacional de Fútbol Profesional, it is one of the premier football leagues in the world, and has been in existence since its formation in 1929.

Consisting of 20 teams, La Liga operates on a system of promotion and relegation with the Segunda División. The season runs from August to May, with each club playing a total of 38 matches (19 at home and 19 away). Teams receive three points for a win, one point for a draw, and no points for a loss, with the rankings determined by total points accumulated.

La Liga has gained a reputation for being one of the best football leagues globally due to its high-quality and technically skilled gameplay. It is particularly known for producing world-class footballers and is home to some of the most successful and popular football clubs in the world, such as Real Madrid, Barcelona, and Atlético Madrid.

La Liga was the first national league to be broadcast in Europe and has since become one of the most widely followed and televised sporting leagues in the world. The league's popularity is bolstered by its high-profile talents, competitive matches, and tactical innovation, making it a significant contributor to the global football industry.

DID YOU KNOW?

The following season, Ronaldo earned his fourth Ballon d'Or, won another La Liga title after five years, secured another Champions League trophy, and achieved his second Club World Cup.

His last season with Real Madrid, 2017-18, was marked by his fifth Ballon d'Or in 2017 and his fifth Champions League title, including scoring twice in the final against Juventus.

DID YOU KNOW?

He transferred to Juventus in July 2018, leaving Real Madrid as its all-time top goal scorer and the only player in La Liga history to score 30 or more goals in six consecutive seasons.

DID YOU KNOW?

Ronaldo set a record as the first player to win the UEFA Champions League five times.

Ronaldo began his international career with Portugal at age 18 and scored his first goal at UEFA Euro 2004, helping Portugal reach the final.

DID YOU KNOW?

He played in his first World Cup in 2006, contributing to Portugal's fourth-place finish.

_____

Ronaldo became the full captain of Portugal in 2008 and has since participated in four European Championships (2008, 2012, 2016, 2020) and three FIFA World Cups (2014, 2018, 2022).

DID YOU KNOW?

During his youth, Cristiano Ronaldo greatly admired Brazilian football legends Ronaldinho and Ronaldo Nazário. He often regarded them as his idols and publicly stated they left "a beautiful history in football."

Ronaldo, celebrated for his lightning speed, has been clocked reaching impressive velocities on the pitch, with recorded speeds of up to 20.9 miles per hour (33.6 kilometers per hour), distinguishing him as one of the fastest football players in the world.

DID YOU KNOW?

Cristiano Ronaldo, while naturally right-footed and exceptionally versatile on the field, capable of playing on both wings and as a striker, says he prefers the forward position, where he can best leverage his prolific goal-scoring skills.

DID YOU KNOW?

Cristiano stands at 6.1 feet tall (1.87 m) and combines his height with an exceptional vertical leap, reportedly measuring up to 30.7 inches (78 cm), which amplifies his already impressive heading ability. This combination makes him a formidable aerial threat in football, capable of out-jumping defenders and goalkeepers alike.

DID YOU KNOW?

Ronaldo is celebrated for mastering the 'knuckleball' free kick technique, where he strikes the ball to minimize spin, causing it to move erratically in the air. This method, difficult for goalkeepers to predict and defend, has led to some spectacular goals. Ronaldo's free kicks often clocked at speeds exceeding 80 miles per hour (130 kilometers per hour).

Ronaldo has scored 140 penalty kicks in his professional club and international career. This figure includes penalties scored for Sporting CP, Manchester United, Real Madrid, Juventus, and the Portugal national team.

DID YOU KNOW?

He has scored 60 hat-tricks in his professional career for club and country.

_____

Cristiano Ronaldo has achieved a remarkable milestone of 807 career goals, surpassing Josef Bican's previous record of 805 goals set between 1931 and 1955, thus establishing Ronaldo as the highest-ever goalscorer in the history of men's soccer.

DID YOU KNOW?

Cristiano Ronaldo's signature "Siu" celebration, a dynamic jump accompanied by a confident shout of "Siu" – meaning "Yes" in Spanish – first debuted in 2013 during a match with Real Madrid against Chelsea in the International Champions Cup, symbolizing his exuberant joy and triumph upon scoring.

DID YOU KNOW?

Cristiano Ronaldo has achieved the remarkable feat of scoring 145 goals with his head across his tenures at five clubs and the Portugal national team.

Ronaldo's astonishing athletic prowess was displayed when he achieved his highest recorded jump of 9 feet 7 inches (2.93m) against Manchester United in the 2012-13 UEFA Champions League while playing for Real Madrid. Given Ronaldo's height of 6 feet 2 inches (1.87m), this jump translates to a remarkable vertical leap of approximately 41.7 inches (1.06m).

DID YOU KNOW?

In 2009, Real Madrid took steps to protect their investment in Ronaldo by insuring his legs for a reported sum of around €100 million.

DID YOU KNOW?

In a Champions League quarter-final match against Juventus, Cristiano Ronaldo scored a stunning bicycle kick goal, widely celebrated as one of the most incredible goals in the tournament's history.

Ronaldo's training regimen, distinguished by its intensity and thoroughness, includes five weekly sessions, each lasting 3 to 4 hours, and encompasses cardio exercises, weight training, football drills, and high-intensity interval training (HIIT) to enhance his speed, strength, agility, and explosive power.

DID YOU KNOW?

Complementing his rigorous workout routine, Ronaldo incorporates core strength exercises, swimming, and Pilates into his regime for balance, recovery, and flexibility. He often exceeds his team's training schedule with additional individual sessions to ensure continuous improvement and peak fitness.

Cristiano's diet, crucial to his training, is meticulously planned with multiple small meals a day, rich in protein, carbohydrates, and healthy fats. He focuses on lean meats, whole grains, fresh fruits, and vegetables while avoiding sugary foods and alcohol to ensure optimal recovery and peak performance.

DID YOU KNOW?

Cristiano Ronaldo incorporates mental exercises, such as meditation and visualization techniques, into his training regimen, enhancing his focus and competitive edge. These practices help him mentally prepare for matches, stay calm under pressure, and visualize successful outcomes, contributing significantly to his on-field performance and decision-making.

Ronaldo is known for his generous philanthropic efforts, notably donating €1.5 million to fund a pediatric hospital in Madeira, his hometown, in 2017.

DID YOU KNOW?

In 2015, Ronaldo was named the world's most charitable sportsperson after donating a substantial amount of money to various causes, including €5 million to the relief efforts following the earthquake in Nepal.

_____

He frequently contributes to children's charities, like Save the Children, and has funded schools in war zones, demonstrating his commitment to improving the lives of underprivileged children.

DID YOU KNOW?

Ronaldo has also been involved in campaigns for blood donation and bone marrow donation, using his global influence to raise awareness about these important causes.

Cristiano has consciously chosen not to have any tattoos on his body, a decision influenced by his commitment to regularly donating blood. By avoiding tattoos, he ensures that he doesn't have to contend with the mandatory waiting periods that can follow tattooing, thus enabling him to donate blood more frequently and continue supporting this vital cause.

DID YOU KNOW?

In response to the COVID-19 pandemic, Ronaldo and his agent, Jorge Mendes, donated significant funds to hospitals in Portugal for critical care beds and medical equipment.

Ronaldo was raised in a devout Catholic family and his faith has been an important aspect of his life. While he is not publicly outspoken about his religious beliefs, he has been known to make gestures on the field that suggest a deep personal faith. For instance, he often makes the cross sign before games, a common practice among Catholic athletes.

DID YOU KNOW?

Cristiano Ronaldo's foray into the world of fragrances is marked by the launch of his signature line, 'CR7 Fragrances.' This collection includes a range of scents designed to reflect Ronaldo's style and charisma. The flagship product, 'CR7 Eau de Toilette,' was first introduced in 2017. It is described as a modern, sporty fragrance with notes of lavender, apple, and cinnamon, making it suitable for everyday wear.

DID YOU KNOW?

In 2003, before rising to global fame, Cristiano Ronaldo appeared in a television commercial for 'Super Bock,' a well-known Portuguese clothing brand. At the time, Ronaldo was just beginning to make his mark in the world of football, and this commercial represented one of his earliest ventures into the realm of brand endorsements.

In 2017, Ronaldo was accused by Spanish authorities of tax evasion, involving €14.7 million in image rights income channeled through offshore companies. He settled the case in 2019, accepting a two-year suspended jail sentence and agreeing to pay €18.8 million in fines, thereby avoiding jail time.

DID YOU KNOW?

Cristiano's intensely competitive nature on the field has led to several red cards and criticism for his behavior, including contentious reactions to referee decisions and confrontations with opponents. His aggressive playing style and occasional dramatics in drawing fouls have sparked debates about sportsmanship in football.

As a global ambassador for Clear Shampoo and Herbalife, Ronaldo uses his widespread popularity to promote hair care and health and wellness products, showcasing his diverse brand appeal.

DID YOU KNOW?

Ronaldo has aligned with TAG Heuer, representing their high-end Swiss watches, and partnered with DAZN, a sports streaming service in the luxury and digital media sectors, to promote their extensive sports coverage.

Expanding his business ventures, Ronaldo has collaborated with American Tourister in the travel industry, co-owns CR7 Hotels in partnership with the Pestana Hotel Group, and endorses MTG's healthcare and fitness products, reflecting his entrepreneurial spirit and commitment to a lifestyle of health and luxury.

DID YOU KNOW?

Cristiano Ronaldo's hair, known for its frequent and varied styles ranging from sleek combed-back looks to edgy spiked designs, has become almost as iconic as his football skills. His zigzag pattern during the 2014 World Cup stood out, trending among fans and media. Often a form of personal expression, his hairstyles are widely imitated globally, enhancing his influence beyond football.

Since 2016, Cristiano Ronaldo has been under a lifetime endorsement deal with Nike, valued at $1 billion. He is the third athlete after LeBron James and Michael Jordan to secure such a significant agreement. Forbes reported that in 2016, Ronaldo's social media presence generated an astounding $474 million in value for Nike through 329 posts, underlining his immense marketing influence.

DID YOU KNOW?

Cristiano's avid interest in luxury vehicles is reflected in his impressive collection of exclusive sports cars, including rare models like the Bugatti Veyron, Lamborghini Aventador, Ferrari F12, and the standout $3 million Bugatti Chiron, known for its exceptional speed and engineering, epitomizing his taste for style and high performance.

DID YOU KNOW?

Ronaldo owns a private jet, which he uses to travel efficiently for professional football matches and personal commitments. This jet allows him the flexibility and convenience to manage his busy schedule, attend various events worldwide, and balance his high-profile career and personal life.

Inaugurated in 2013, the CR7 Museum in Cristiano Ronaldo's birthplace of Funchal, Madeira, is a tribute to the soccer star's illustrious career and life. The museum showcases a comprehensive collection, including photographs from Ronaldo's childhood and his accumulated trophies, medals, and even soccer balls from notable matches.

DID YOU KNOW?

Ronaldo has scored 60 free-kick goals in his professional career. His 'knuckleball' free-kick technique makes the ball move unpredictably in flight, challenging goalkeepers.

In 2020, he made history by becoming the first active team-sport athlete to surpass $1 billion in career earnings, as reported by Forbes.

DID YOU KNOW?

Cristiano Ronaldo's relationship with Georgina Rodriguez began in 2016 when they first met at a Gucci store in Madrid. Georgina worked as a shop assistant at 22 while Ronaldo was 31.

DID YOU KNOW?

Cristiano's family includes his first child, Cristiano Jr., born in June 2010, over whom Ronaldo has full custody, with the mother's identity kept private. In June 2017, he expanded his family by welcoming twins Eva and Mateo, who were born via surrogacy.

In 2017, Ronaldo's family grew once more when his partner, Georgina Rodriguez, gave birth to their daughter Alana Martina in November, marking Ronaldo's fourth child.

DID YOU KNOW?

Cristiano Ronaldo strongly emphasizes family values, consistently highlighting their importance in his life. He frequently dedicates quality time to his children and partner, engaging in simple yet meaningful activities such as playing games and relaxing together at home.

Cristiano Ronaldo has a penchant for traveling to various stunning destinations worldwide. His favorite vacation spots have included Ibiza, Miami, Dubai, Paris, Madeira (his hometown), Greece, Las Vegas, and the Maldives. These destinations offer a glimpse into his diverse travel interests, from vibrant nightlife to tropical paradises, reflecting his love for exploration and relaxation.

DID YOU KNOW?

Cristiano Ronaldo actively participates in prominent fashion events, including fashion weeks in cities like Paris and Milan, and gatherings hosted by renowned brands like Dolce & Gabbana and Versace.

DID YOU KNOW?

He has actively participated in professional poker tournaments and promotional poker events. However, no widely reported significant poker winnings are associated with his involvement. His interest in poker is more about enjoyment and brand promotion rather than substantial monetary gains.

Cristiano frequently attends concerts by artists such as Rihanna and Jennifer Lopez, sharing his music preferences on social media. His global prominence has also resulted in collaborations with musicians, exemplified by his appearances in music videos and promotional campaigns, like those for Ricky Martin.

DID YOU KNOW?

Ronaldo has shared the pitch with several notable players, including Wayne Rooney, Ryan Giggs, and Paul Scholes, during his time at Manchester United, forming a formidable partnership that contributed to multiple Premier League titles and Champions League success.

At Real Madrid, Ronaldo played alongside Sergio Ramos, Luka Modrić, and Karim Benzema, achieving great success. His international rivalry with Lionel Messi has also produced iconic clashes when representing Portugal and Argentina.

DID YOU KNOW?

Ronaldo signed a two-and-a-half year contract estimated by media to be worth more than 200 million euros ($220.16 million) with Al Nassr and made his debut in January 2023.

Throughout his career, Ronaldo has faced a series of significant injuries and setbacks, including an ankle injury during the 2008 UEFA European Championship, a knee injury while at Real Madrid in 2014, a thigh injury in 2019 while playing for Juventus, and a period of COVID-19 isolation in 2020. In each instance, Ronaldo showcased his resilience and determination, swiftly recovering and returning to the field to maintain his high level of performance.

DID YOU KNOW?

He boasts the most-viewed Wikipedia page for a male athlete, with a staggering 112 million views. He is also the fourth most followed person on Twitter, with 110 million followers.

Ronaldo's mentorship extends to nurturing young and lesser-known talents at Manchester United and Real Madrid. His guidance and belief in players like Danny Welbeck, Federico Macheda, Lucas Vázquez, and Marco Asensio have been instrumental in their development, boosting their confidence and helping them thrive in top-level football.

DID YOU KNOW?

Cristiano Ronaldo's close friends among famous personalities include former Manchester United teammates Patrice Evra and Rio Ferdinand, UFC fighter Conor McGregor, and Hollywood actor Dwayne 'The Rock' Johnson.

Cristiano Ronaldo is proficient in several languages beyond Portuguese, including English, Spanish, and Italian. These language skills have facilitated his international football career and allowed him to connect with fans and teammates from different backgrounds and cultures.

DID YOU KNOW?

Known for his accessibility, Ronaldo often grants fans requests for selfies and autographs, making time for personal interactions at training sessions, airports, and public events. He engages actively with his global fan base on social media, personally responding to comments and messages, strengthening his connection with supporters worldwide.

DID YOU KNOW?

Ronaldo has made a substantial community impact in his hometown of Madeira, Portugal, through donations to the local hospital, the creation of the CR7 Museum, youth development programs, and charitable work via the Cristiano Ronaldo Foundation. His efforts have positively influenced the region's healthcare, tourism, education, and youth empowerment.

Cristiano is an animal lover who owns several dog breeds, including bulldogs and labrador retrievers, frequently sharing his affection for his canine companions on social media.

DID YOU KNOW?

Ronaldo's early mentors were instrumental in his football journey. Sporting CP provided essential guidance during his formative years, while at Manchester United, legendary manager Sir Alex Ferguson coached and mentored him. Additionally, Carlos Queiroz, the assistant manager at Manchester United, played a vital role in Ronaldo's development as a top-level footballer through coaching and guidance.

In FIFA 18, Ronaldo held the top spot as the highest-rated player with an impressive overall rating of 99%, placing him 1% ahead of runners-up Lionel Messi and Pelé, who both had ratings of 98%.

DID YOU KNOW?

Cristiano's legendary association with the number 7 jersey has left an indelible mark on his career. At Manchester United, he inherited this iconic number, previously worn by club legends like George Best, Eric Cantona, and David Beckham.

DID YOU KNOW?

Famous for his meticulous nature, Ronaldo adheres to a set of superstitious habits. These rituals range from stepping onto the pitch with his right foot to carefully styling his hair before every match, all of which have become integral components of his pre-game routine.

Upon his arrival at Manchester United in 2003, Cristiano Ronaldo had a limited grasp of English. He required a translator to communicate with his manager, Sir Alex Ferguson. Ronaldo humorously remarked that even to this day, he finds it challenging to understand Ferguson's Scottish accent. In the early days, he relied on a Brazilian translator primarily for interactions with his manager.

DID YOU KNOW?

Cristiano became the fourth footballer to be represented as a waxwork at Madame Tussauds in London. He joined the ranks of other football legends like Steven Gerrard, Pelé, and David Beckham, who had also been honored with wax figures at the famous museum. These wax statues are created to commemorate the achievements and popularity of notable individuals in various fields, including sports.

Ronaldo holds the record as the most-followed individual, male figure, sports personality, and European personality on Instagram, boasting an impressive following of over 612 million users.

DID YOU KNOW?

Throughout his distinguished career, Cristiano has continually evolved his playing style, starting as a winger at Manchester United, where he focused on delivering crosses, then transitioning to a more central striker role at Real Madrid with an emphasis on goal-scoring, and finally at Juventus, where he combined his role as a prolific target man with a return to more active dribbling and crossing, occasionally revisiting his roots as a winger to engage defenders directly. Ronaldo has stated his ambition to continue playing football at the highest level well into his late 30s, demonstrating his commitment to maintaining peak physical condition and performance.

TRIVIA QUESTIONS!

1) What is Cristiano Ronaldo's full name?
a) Cristiano Ronaldo Aveiro
b) Cristiano Ronaldo dos Santos Aveiro
c) Cristiano Ronaldo Silva
d) Cristiano Ronaldo Fernandez

2) Who was Ronaldo's role model and the inspiration behind his name?
a) Lionel Messi
b) Cristiano Ronaldo Sr.
c) Ronaldinho
d) Ronald Reagan

3) What was Cristiano Ronaldo's nickname as a child due to his speed?
a) Little Bee
b) Speedy Gonzales
c) Flash
d) Bolt

4) At what age did Cristiano Ronaldo start playing football for Andorinha?
a) 8
b) 10
c) 12
d) 14

TRIVIA QUESTIONS!

5) What medical condition did Cristiano Ronaldo undergo heart surgery for at the age of 15?
a) Broken arm
b) Tachycardia
c) Asthma
d) Migraine

6) In which year did Cristiano Ronaldo make his professional debut for Sporting CP?
a) 2000
b) 2002
c) 2004
d) 2006

7) Which club signed Cristiano Ronaldo for a then-record fee of £12.24 million when he was 18 years old?
a) FC Barcelona
b) Manchester United
c) Real Madrid
d) Sporting CP

8) What was Cristiano Ronaldo's signature move, known for outmaneuvering defenders?
a) Bicycle Kick
b) Rainbow Flick
c) Ronaldo Chop
d) Scorpion Kick

TRIVIA QUESTIONS!

9) During his time at Manchester United, in which season did Cristiano Ronaldo help the club secure the UEFA Champions League title?
a) 2005-06
b) 2006-07
c) 2007-08
d) 2008-09

10) What was the world-record transfer fee when Cristiano Ronaldo transferred from Manchester United to Real Madrid in 2009?
a) £40 million
b) £60 million
c) £80 million
d) £100 million

11) In which season did Cristiano Ronaldo win his second Ballon d'Or award?
a) 2011-12
b) 2012-13
c) 2013-14
d) 2014-15

12) How many UEFA Champions League titles did Ronaldo win during his time with Real Madrid?
a) 2
b) 3
c) 4
d) 5

TRIVIA QUESTIONS!

13) When did Cristiano Ronaldo become the full captain of the Portugal national team?
a) 2004
b) 2006
c) 2008
d) 2010

14) Who were Cristiano Ronaldo's idols and football legends during his youth?
a) Diego Maradona and Pelé
b) Lionel Messi and Neymar
c) Ronaldinho and Ronaldo Nazário
d) Zinedine Zidane and David Beckham

15) What is Cristiano Ronaldo's preferred position on the field?
a) Midfielder
b) Defender
c) Forward
d) Goalkeeper

16) What is the fastest recorded speed that Cristiano Ronaldo reached on the pitch?
a) 18.5 miles per hour
b) 20.9 miles per hour
c) 22.5 miles per hour
d) 24.3 miles per hour

TRIVIA QUESTIONS!

17) How many career goals has Cristiano Ronaldo scored with his head?
a) 50
b) 75
c) 100
d) 145

18) What is the significance of Cristiano Ronaldo's "Siu" celebration?
a) It means "No" in Spanish
b) It symbolizes victory and joy
c) It's a tribute to his favorite football club
d) It's a message to his teammates

19) What record did Cristiano Ronaldo set in the UEFA Champions League?
a) Most assists in a single season
b) Most goals in a single season
c) Most consecutive hat-tricks
d) Most penalties scored

20) How many hat-tricks has Cristiano Ronaldo scored in his professional career for club and country?
a) 30
b) 45
c) 60
d) 75

TRIVIA QUESTIONS!

21) How many weekly training sessions does Cristiano Ronaldo typically undergo?
a) 4
b) 5
c) 6
d) 7

22) What type of training is NOT part of Cristiano Ronaldo's workout regimen?
a) Weight training
b) Swimming
c) Yoga
d) High-intensity interval training (HIIT)

23) What does Ronaldo primarily focus on in his diet to support his training?
a) Sugary foods and alcohol
b) Lean meats and whole grains
c) Processed snacks and fast food
d) Carbonated beverages and fried foods

24) Besides physical exercises, what other techniques does Cristiano Ronaldo incorporate into his training regimen?
a) Cooking lessons
b) Meditation and visualization
c) Dancing
d) Singing

TRIVIA QUESTIONS!

25) In 2017, Cristiano Ronaldo donated €1.5 million to fund what in his hometown of Madeira?
a) A soccer stadium
b) A pediatric hospital
c) A school for the arts
d) A public library

26) What major natural disaster prompted Cristiano Ronaldo to donate €5 million to relief efforts in 2015?
a) Hurricane
b) Earthquake in Nepal
c) Tsunami
d) Tornado

27) Which cause has Cristiano Ronaldo NOT been involved in campaigning for?
a) Blood donation
b) Bone marrow donation
c) Cancer research
d) Child welfare

28) Why has Cristiano Ronaldo chosen not to have tattoos on his body?
a) He is afraid of needles
b) He doesn't like the look of tattoos
c) To avoid mandatory waiting periods for blood donation
d) To stand out from other football players

TRIVIA QUESTIONS!

29) What significant donation did Cristiano Ronaldo and his agent Jorge Mendes make in response to the COVID-19 pandemic?
a) Donated ventilators to hospitals
b) Funded a new vaccine research center
c) Supported critical care beds and medical equipment in Portugal
d) Provided free masks to the public

30) What gesture does Cristiano Ronaldo often make before games, reflecting his faith?
a) Saluting the crowd
b) Kissing the ball
c) Making the cross sign
d) Doing a cartwheel

31) How many children does Cristiano Ronaldo have?
a) 2
b) 3
c) 4
d) 5

32) When were Cristiano Ronaldo's twins, Eva and Mateo, born?
a) June 2010
b) June 2017
c) November 2017
d) July 2018

TRIVIA QUESTIONS!

33) Who is Cristiano Ronaldo's partner and the mother of his daughter Alana Martina?
a) Georgina Rodriguez
b) Irina Shayk
c) Alessandra Ambrosio
d) Shakira

34) What significant financial milestone did Cristiano Ronaldo achieve in 2020?
a) $100 million in career earnings
b) $500 million in career earnings
c) $1 billion in career earnings
d) $10 billion in career earnings

35) Which of the following destinations is NOT mentioned as one of Cristiano Ronaldo's favorite vacation spots?
a) Ibiza
b) Paris
c) Moscow
d) Maldives

36) In addition to football, Cristiano Ronaldo actively participates in which other area of interest?
a) Professional poker
b) Cooking
c) Chess
d) Painting

TRIVIA QUESTIONS!

37) Which artists have Cristiano Ronaldo publicly mentioned attending concerts of?
a) Elvis Presley and Frank Sinatra
b) Rihanna and Jennifer Lopez
c) The Beatles and Queen
d) Beyoncé and Justin Bieber

38) During his time at Manchester United, which players formed a notable partnership with Cristiano Ronaldo?
a) Lionel Messi and Neymar
b) Wayne Rooney and Ryan Giggs
c) Sergio Ramos and Luka Modrić
d) Zinedine Zidane and David Beckham

39) How has Cristiano Ronaldo demonstrated his resilience and determination in his career?
a) By becoming a professional poker champion
b) By consistently avoiding injuries
c) By swiftly recovering from injuries and setbacks
d) By switching to a career in music

40) Cristiano Ronaldo's signature celebration, where he jumps and shouts "Siu," first debuted in 2013 during a match with which club?
a) Manchester United
b) Real Madrid
c) Sporting CP
d) Juventus

TRIVIA ANSWERS!

1. b) Cristiano Ronaldo dos Santos Aveiro
2. d) Ronald Reagan
3. a) Little Bee
4. a) 8
5. b) Tachycardia
6. b) 2002
7. b) Manchester United
8. c) Ronaldo Chop
9. c) 2007-08
10. c) £80 million

11. b) 2012-13
12. c) 4
13. c) 2008
14. c) Ronaldinho and Ronaldo Nazário
15. c) Forward
16. b) 20.9 miles per hour
17. d) 145
18. b) It symbolizes victory and joy
19. b) Most goals in a single season
20. c) 60

TRIVIA ANSWERS!

21. b) 5
22. c) Yoga
23. b) Lean meats and whole grains
24. b) Meditation and visualization
25. b) A pediatric hospital
26. b) Earthquake in Nepal
27. c) Cancer research
28. c) To avoid mandatory waiting periods for blood donation
29. c) Supported critical care beds and medical equipment in Portugal
30. c) Making the cross sign

31. c) 4
32. b) June 2017
33. a) Georgina Rodriguez
34. c) $1 billion in career earnings
35. c) Moscow
36. a) Professional poker
37. b) Rihanna and Jennifer Lopez
38. b) Wayne Rooney and Ryan Giggs
39. c) By swiftly recovering from injuries and setbacks
40. b) Real Madrid

SCORE ___/40

16-20: Room for Improvement
You're on the right track, but there's more to discover about Ronaldo. Keep learning, and you'll get better!

21-25: Not Bad!
You've got a fair understanding of Cristiano Ronaldo. Keep exploring, and you'll improve even more!

26-30: Good Going!
You know quite a bit about Ronaldo. Keep learning and you'll become an expert in no time!

31-35: Great Job!
You've got a fantastic knowledge of Cristiano Ronaldo. Keep up the good work!

36-40: You're a Pro!
Wow, you really know Cristiano Ronaldo inside out. You're a true Ronaldo expert!

JOURNAL PAGES

JOURNAL PAGES

JOURNAL PAGES

JOURNAL PAGES

JOURNAL PAGES

WANT A FREE BOOK ON MESSI?

Are you ready to delve into the next thrilling book in the series, absolutely free? Get ready to explore the captivating world of yet another football legend!

Just use your smartphone or tablet to scan the QR code below, then follow the simple prompts to receive the PDF.

Made in United States
Orlando, FL
09 December 2024

55261341R00055